THE FURRY HISTORY OF CATS

Clive Gifford and
Andressa Meissner

W
FRANKLIN WATTS
LONDON · SYDNEY

First published in Great Britain in 2025 by Hodder & Stoughton
© Hodder & Stoughton Limited, 2025.

All rights reserved

Managing editor: Victoria Brooker / Design: Gemma Steward
Consultant: Briony Smith, Curator at The Big Cat Sanctuary

ISBN: 9781445190556 (hbk) / ISBN: 9781445190570 (pbk) / 9781445190563 (ebk)

Printed in Dubai

Franklin Watts, an imprint of Hachette Children's Group
Part of Hodder & Stoughton
Carmelite House, 50 Victoria Embankment, London EC4Y 0DZ

An Hachette UK Company
www.hachette.co.uk
www.hachettechildrens.co.uk

The authorised representative in the EEA is Hachette Ireland, 8 Castlecourt Centre, Dublin 15, D15 XTP3, Ireland (email: info@hbgi.ie)

MIX
Paper | Supporting responsible forestry
FSC® C104740

CONTENTS

Roarsome and Awesome	4
Prehistoric Cats	6
Meet The Family	8
Cat Anatomy	10
Paw-fect Senses	12
Furry Nice!	14
Feline Behaviour	16
Cubs and Kittens	18
Amazing Adaptations	20
Lions	22
Tigers	24
Cheetahs	26
Jaguars	28
Leopards and Snow Leopards	30
More Cats	32
Domestic Cats	34
Cats And Humans	36
Cats in Crisis	38
Losing Their Homes	40
Cat Studies	42
Cat Conservation	44
Glossary	46
Further Information	47
Index	48

ROARSOME AND AWESOME

From a pouncing puma to the cutest kitty, cats are amongst the most intriguing and much-loved mammals on the planet. They live in the wild on all continents except Oceania and Antarctica.

There are 40 species of different cats, ranging from wild cats smaller than the domestic pet cats found in many homes to large, powerful beasts like lions, tigers and jaguars.

Wild cats can be found living in snowy mountains and sweltering jungles. Some are expert climbers or swimmers, others rely on their sheer power or speed to catch their prey.

Beautiful clouded leopards live in Nepal, India, China and south-east Asia. They are expert climbers and can even hang upside-down beneath large branches.

The clouded leopard eats deer, porcupines and monkeys.

Found in southern Africa, the tiny black-footed cat weighs just a third of a domestic cat and cannot climb well. Despite this, it's the most efficient cat hunter, catching 60 per cent of its intended prey. It can eat up to 14 small creatures – from locusts to gerbils – each night.

The black-footed cat can leap up to 1.4 m into the air to catch a bird in mid-flight.

Pampas cat

Pampas cats' habitats include the woodlands and grasslands of South America. There, they hunt small mammals. They've even been observed stealing penguin eggs.

PREHISTORIC CATS

The story of cats begins more than 25–33 million years ago when the first cat-like species are thought to have evolved. Fossils of many early species, like *Proailurus*, were small – around one-and-a-half to two times the size of a modern domestic cat.

Pseudaelurus

Pseudaelurus, however, was bigger, weighing up to 30 kg or so. Fossils of this cat have been found in Europe, North America and Asia.

Species of sabre-toothed cats with giant canine teeth evolved later. The most famous are the three species of *Smilodon* that lived from 2.58 million years up until 11,200 years ago. The largest, *S. populator*, stood around 120 cm high and may have weighed over 400 kg – that's the weight of a large tiger PLUS two adult people.

Smilodon gracilis

Smilodon fatalis

Smilodon populator

Smilodon's top two canine teeth were up to 25 cm long and curved wickedly. Experts think that it would plunge them deep into a creature's neck or body, cutting blood vessels and causing a severe wound.

Tapir

Giant ground sloth

A *Smilodon*'s jaw had to open extremely wide to make use of its giant canine teeth.

Smilodon populator

Bison

These big cats roamed the prehistoric forests and open woodlands of the Americas. The cat was stocky with a muscular neck and short but very powerful legs. Scientists think it would not have chased prey out in the open; rather, it would hide and pounce, using its meaty front paws to pin down creatures like tapirs, giant ground sloths and woodland bison.

MEET THE FAMILY

All cats are felids – they are all part of one big family called *Felidae*. Scientists then split them up into two sub-families: the *Felinae* or smaller cats and the *Pantherinae* or big cats.

PANTHERINAE

Pantherinae cats began evolving into their different species about 10.8 million years ago. Today, they consist of the lion, tiger, jaguar, leopard, snow leopard and two species of clouded leopard. All of these cats can roar ... except the clouded leopards.

EVOLUTION OF THE CAT

Marbled cat

BAY CAT LINEAGE
Asian golden cat
Marbled cat

CARACAL LINEAGE
Caracal
Serval

Serval

LEOPARDUS LINEAGE
Ocelot
Pampas cat

Ocelot

LYNX LINEAGE
Iberian lynx
Bobcat

Bobcat

PUMA LINEAGE
Jaguarundi
Cheetah

LEOPARD CAT LINEAGE
Pallas's cat
Flat-headed cat

Pallas's cat

DOMESTIC CAT LINEAGE
European wildcat
Sand cat

Sand cat

FELINAE
There are seven different *Felinae* lineages. Scientists think that the first to evolve was the bay cat lineage which contains marbled cats, bay cats and the Asian golden cat, about 9.4 million years ago.

The cheetah is grouped in the puma lineage with the lesser-known South American cat called the jaguarundi.

The jaguarundi feeds on small reptiles, rodents and birds on the ground.

Jaguarundi

The last to evolve was the lineage that includes domesticated or house cats that many people keep as pets. This lineage began around 3.4 million years ago with the domesticated cat its newest member.

9

CAT ANATOMY

Cat species may vary greatly in size but have much in common. Certain features of their bodies, including strong shoulder muscles and lightweight skeletons, help give all cats their agile movement and great hunting prowess.

The scruff is a very loose area of skin at the back of the neck. It is where mother cats grip their kittens or cubs with their teeth.

The head is short and doesn't have a long snout or muzzle like dogs or wolves. Most species have large eyes that point forwards giving them sharp vision.

Whiskers

Mouth contains 30 teeth (or 28 in a lynx) mostly used for grasping and tearing.

A cat's paws have well-padded soles and five toes on the front paws with four toes on the rear paws. Cats are digitgrades which means they walk on their toes.

The heart pumps blood around the body. A domestic cat's heart beats 140-220 times a minute.

BIG PAWS
The Canada lynx has particularly large paws for its size. It splays these out wide to use them like snowshoes when padding through soft snow in Arctic forests in North America.

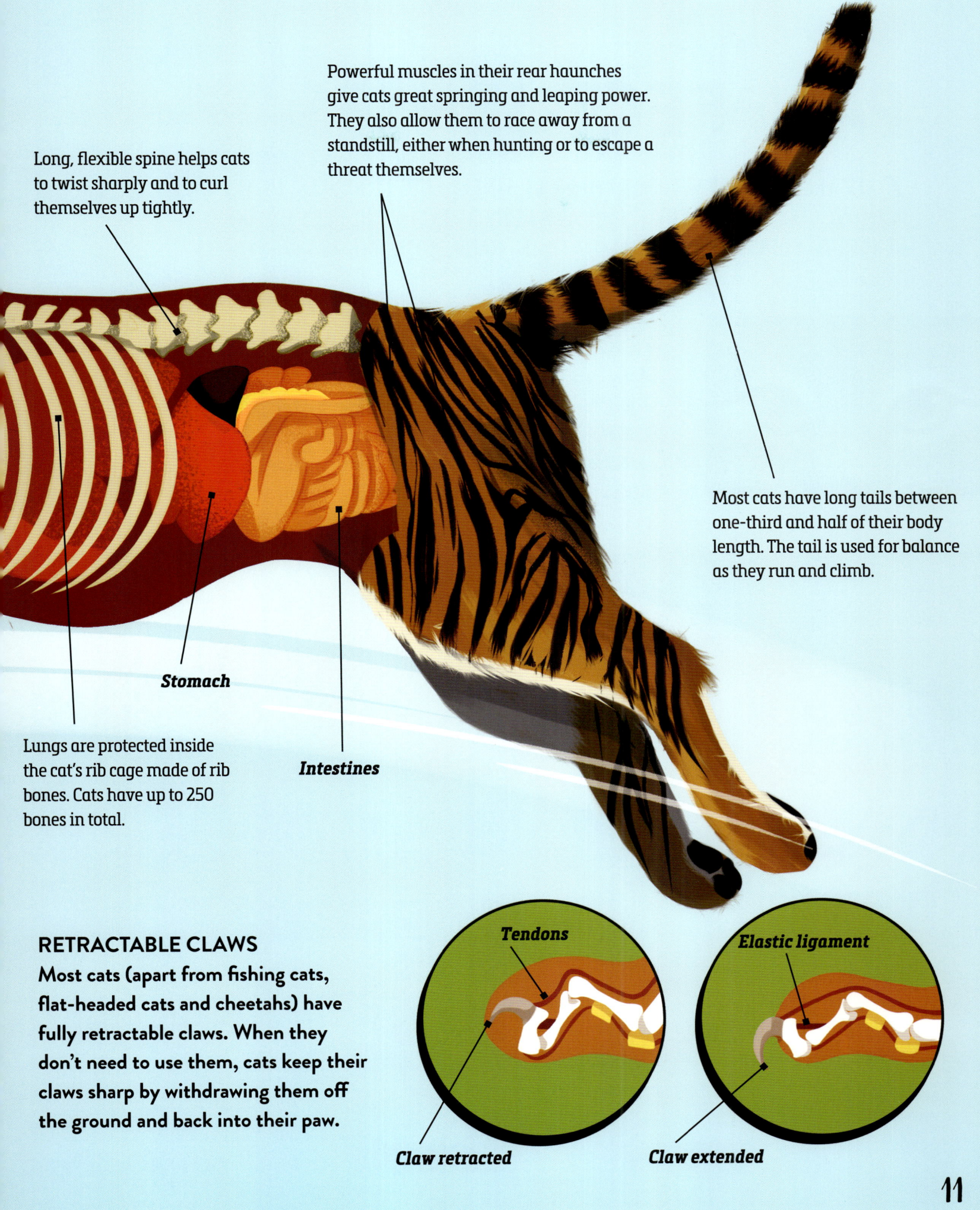

PAW-FECT SENSES

Cats are equipped with a number of finely-honed senses. In the wild, most cats live on their own and hunt at night, so rely on their senses to survive and thrive in a wide range of habitats.

VISION
Many cats see well in the dark. A tiger's night vision, for example, is around six times better than humans. Most smaller cat species have oval-shaped pupils which can shrink to vertical slits to help detect tiny movements.

All cats have a shiny membrane at the back of their eyes called the *tapetum lucidum*. It reflects light and improves their vision in dim conditions. It makes a cat's eyes shine eerily when a light strikes them.

HEARING

Cats' hearing is more sensitive than humans and can detect higher-pitched sounds than us. Muscles turn their ears (up to 180° in some species) to focus on the direction sounds are coming from.

A serval's oversized ears can detect the smallest sound made by the rats and mice it hunts. If your ears were the same proportion to your body as a serval's, they would be the size of dinner plates!

SMELL

Cats use smell to detect food, other cats and animals, identifying them as friend or foe. This sense is enhanced by the Jacobson's organ which opens in the roof of a cat's mouth so it can 'taste' smells.

TOUCH

Whiskers are long stiff hairs embedded in skin packed with nerve endings. They are as wide as the cat, allowing it to judge whether its body can squeeze through a narrow space. Whiskers sense temperature and vibrations in the air – really useful for measuring distances or stalking prey.

FURRY NICE!

Some domestic cats like the Sphynx have been bred to have fur-free bodies. All other cats are covered in layers of closely packed hairs that form fur. This keeps them warm and dry, protects against the Sun's harmful rays and acts as camouflage – hiding them amongst their surroundings.

A clouded leopard's markings help camouflage it in its mangrove swamp and lowland tropical forest habitats.

Different types of hair make up a cat's fur. Oily guard hairs form the top layer or coat of fur. These repel water, give the cat its appearance and are sensitive to pressure. They also work with a cat's whiskers to help cats judge spaces and close-up distances accurately.

The layer closest to their skin is known as down hair and forms the underfur. This layer insulates the cat, keeping heat in and the cold out.

The Pallas's Cat lives in colder regions of central Asia where temperatures can drop below -30ºC. Its fur is the longest and densest of any cat in relation to body size, with as many as 9,000 hairs each square centimetre.

SPOTS, STRIPES, ROSETTES

Different species have their own distinctive fur patterns. Lions are plain coloured, tigers have their stripes, cheetahs have their spots. Some cats have all three! The fishing cat, for example, has grey fur with stripes on the shoulders, a plain white belly and spots on its sides.

Tiger

Cheetah

Leopard

Ocelot

Margay

Jaguar

Fishing cat

Some cats, including leopards, ocelots, margays and jaguars, have roundish markings called rosettes because they look a little like a rose flower. These markings help disguise them when hunting or hiding.

FELINE BEHAVIOUR

Pet cats display many of the same behaviours as their wild relatives – from purring, rolling and stretching to finding something to sharpen their claws on. All cats rest a lot, sleeping in a series of shortish naps often for more than half of each 24 hour day.

SCENT AND SPRAYING

Cats have a number of scent glands around their bodies. Domestic cats often rub their scent on their owners, marking them as well as household objects as part of their territory.

Cats will often mix their urine with a fatty marking scent from glands near their tail. They spray trees and other parts of their territory with the mixture. This scent is only detectable by other cats and may last for many days.

A tiger sprays a tree trunk and will re-mark the same location regularly. Tiger urine smells remarkably like buttered popcorn!

Many cats use the back of their paw like a flannel, licking it then rubbing it across their face.

RIGHTING REFLEX

Cats' extraordinarily flexible spines lets them twist in the air to land on their feet safely after a fall. The vestibular apparatus inside a cat's inner ear helps cats orientate themselves when falling. It lets them know which way is up, allowing them to rapidly rotate their head and body into an upright position for a safe landing.

GROOMING

Cats like to be clean. Many spend around a third of their time awake grooming themselves. They use their tongue which is covered in hard spiny bumps called papillae. These point backwards and are used to scrape meat off bones when eating. During grooming, they are used to comb fur clean.

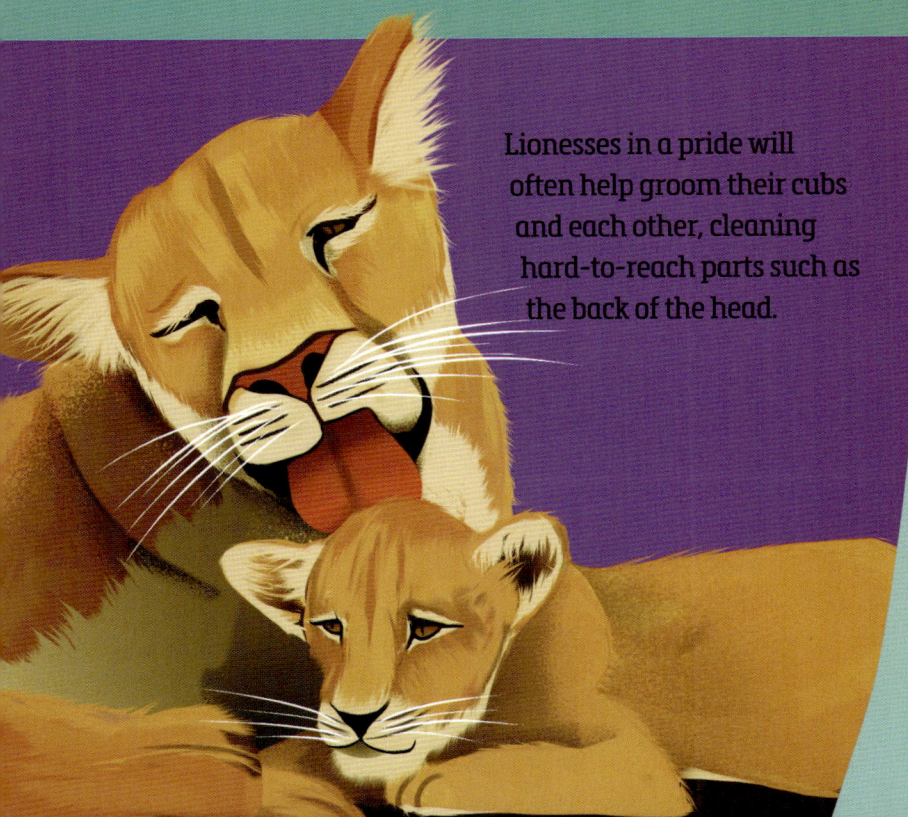

Lionesses in a pride will often help groom their cubs and each other, cleaning hard-to-reach parts such as the back of the head.

CUBS AND KITTENS

It takes 56–115 days, depending on the species, for a cat to be conceived, develop inside its mother and be born. The young of big cats are called cubs and the young of smaller species, like domestic cats, are known as kittens.

All cats are born tiny, blind and unable to fend for themselves. A European wildcat weighs 65–160 g at birth and a baby cheetah weighs 15–350 g. Cubs and kittens gain their sight within a couple of weeks and grow up fast, aided by guzzling their mother's milk.

They stay close to their mother for food and protection in their first months as they are weaned off milk and start eating meat. A parent may carry a straying cub or kitten in its mouth, holding the infant by the scruff of its neck.

As they grow, cubs and kittens play and play-fight with each other, learning and honing vital stalking, pouncing and chasing skills. Their mother may also teach them hunting skills as well.

In the wild, many cubs and kittens don't reach adulthood. Many threats exist including disease, starvation and being trampled by larger animals. Other creatures sometimes hunt cubs and kittens including swooping birds of prey and, in some cases, adult males of their own species!

Those that do survive will eventually leave their mother's protection and find their own territory to roam. European wildcats, for example, leave after about five months whilst tigers stay with their mother for 18–24 months.

AMAZING ADAPTATIONS

All wild cats, big and small, survive and thrive by hunting other creatures. Each species, though, has different adaptations and behaviour based on their diet and habitat. Some are quite unusual, as proven by the following four cats.

The margay lives in the Amazon rainforest and is a nimble climber with soft, broad paw pads for good grip. If it falls from a branch, it can grab hold of another branch with a single paw. Margays are also incredible impressionists. They mimic the call of a baby pied tamarin monkey to lure adult pied tamarins towards them so they can pounce.

The sand cat lives in the Sahara Desert, the Arabian Peninsula and the deserts of central Asia. It can go without water for weeks, getting the moisture it needs from the food it eats. It grows dense fur on the soles of its paws to protect it from hot sand and rock and can dig down quickly to reach prey buried in the sand.

Sand cats are fearless hunters of desert snakes as well as spiders, rodents and insects.

The long legs and neck of servals allow them to peer over the tall plants in the grasslands they inhabit. Servals have excellent hearing, courtesy of their over-sized ears (see page 13) and use their long limbs to spring sharply up to 2 m into the air before pouncing straight down onto their small prey.

The flat-headed cat lives near water in South-East Asia and Indonesia. Fish form a major part of its diet and its teeth point backwards into its mouth to keep a firm grip of slippery prey.

Webs between its toes turn its paws into paddles making them quick movers in water.

LIONS

Lions once lived right across Europe and Asia (as well as Africa) but now they are the African savannah's most famous inhabitant. There is also a small population of Asiatic lions found in the Gir Forest National Park in India.

Lions are impressively built with broad chests, big paws and powerful muscles. Males can grow over 2 m long (head to body) and weigh 160–220 kg. A striking feature of most male lions are the hairy mane which frames their head. The mane can grow up to 16 cm long and gets darker the older the lion gets.

Lions hunt larger African mammals such as zebra, antelope and wildebeest. Lionesses do most of the work and often hunt together to bring down larger prey such as buffalo or smaller giraffes or elephants.

Adult lions need 5–7 kg of meat a day to survive but may eat 30 kg or more in a single meal. Younger male lions may guard the remains of a large kill in between meals whilst the rest of the pride rest after feasting.

Many big cats live solitary lives but lions are different. Most live as part of a social group of 12–30 animals called a pride. Lion cubs are brought up socially and may suckle milk from different lionesses in the pride. The pride mark their territory and may all roar together. A group roar can be heard 8 km away.

TIGERS

The biggest and most powerful of all the big cats, tigers once roamed much of Asia. There are now less than 6,000 of these majestic creatures in the wild, over half of which are found in India.

Tigers are strong with heavy bodies, powerful legs and big paws. Tiger cubs are born weighing 800-1,600 g – less than human babies – but grow up fast. An adult male tiger can weigh up to 270 kg – about four times the weight of a man.

Unlike lions, tigers are solitary hunters. They sleep up to 15 or 16 hours a day. Their vertical stripes camouflage them amongst the undergrowth. No two tigers have the exact same set of body markings.

After dusk, tigers prowl as much as 20 km per night. They use their soft footpads to tread quietly to avoid detection by their prey which they locate and track using their keen eyesight and hearing.

Tigers stalk mostly deer and wild boar, but will also hunt turtles, baby rhinos, buffalo and even leopards. Only around one in ten of their hunting attempts succeed, but a larger kill can keep a tiger well-fed for a week.

Tigers will often cover the remains of a kill with dirt and leaves, hiding it until they are hungry again.

SIBERIAN TIGER
Found in eastern Russia and northern China, Amur tigers, formerly known as Siberian tigers, are the largest big cats. They can grow up to 3.3 m long and weigh as much as 260 kg in winter.

CHEETAHS

Found in Africa's grasslands, with a tiny population living wild in Iran, the cheetah is the world's fastest land animal. They can go from 0–50 km/h in just three strides, and sprint at speeds above 80–100 km/h ... but only over short distances.

From head to tail, cheetahs are especially adapted for high speed pursuit of smaller African hooved animals such as antelope, impala and gazelle. Their head is small and streamlined with big nostrils to let in as much air as possible (a cheetah will take up to 150 breaths a minute when sprinting). Their oversized lungs and heart, which can beat up to 240 times a minute, pump blood and oxygen around their body.

A cheetah's lightweight skeleton includes a long, flexible spine which, coupled with long legs, allows it to take giant bounds, each covering 6–7 m. Their paws are small with their claws extended and are used for grip and traction when running, a little like an athlete's running spikes.

Their tail is stretched out when running fast and helps keep them balanced. It can act like a rudder to help them turn as they chase prey.

Cheetahs tend to hunt in the daytime when other big cats and predators are less active. They bite the neck of their prey and tend to eat immediately then abandon their kill. Sometimes, they will chase and eat ground-dwelling birds and rabbits.

JAGUARS

The third biggest cat, after the tiger and lion, jaguars grow up to 1.7 m long and can weigh as much as 120 kg. It is the largest cat found in the Americas and was once found roaming from the southern United States all the way to southern Argentina.

Today, jaguars occupy a much smaller range with around half found in Brazil in the Amazon rainforest or the Pantanal wetlands. They spend much of their time close to water and, unlike many cats, are excellent swimmers.

Sloth

This strong big cat gets its name from the native American word, *yaguar*. *Yaguar* means, 'he who kills with one leap'. With their short, stocky legs, they are powerful jumpers and frequently climb trees. They also use their claws to mark trees to indicate their territory.

In ancient civilisations like the Olmecs, Maya and Aztecs, the jaguar was a symbol of power and protection.

Jaguars are threatened by habitat loss as large areas of forest are cleared for farmland or ranches.

Jaguars have an extremely powerful bite. Their teeth can pierce the shell of river turtles or the skull of creatures like monkeys, deer and capybaras. They will also hunt fish, birds and even tackle fearsome predators like the caiman and prey as big as a tapir.

Tapir

LEOPARDS

Leopards are mostly found in wooded grasslands in Africa and southern Asia. A small number of Amur leopards are found in the forests of eastern Russia. Adults live solitary lives. Their rosette-patterned fur camouflages them well in trees whilst their roar is raspy like a saw cutting wood.

Leopards have one of the most varied diets of wild cats, eating everything from dung beetles and fish to antelopes and baboons. They ambush prey often through powerful leaps and can sprint in short bursts up to 60 km/h.

They are skilled climbers and may spend the day resting on a tree branch before hunting at dusk or night. They even use trees as larders, dragging the body of a creature bigger than them up a tree to keep it away from other carnivores on the ground looking for an easy meal.

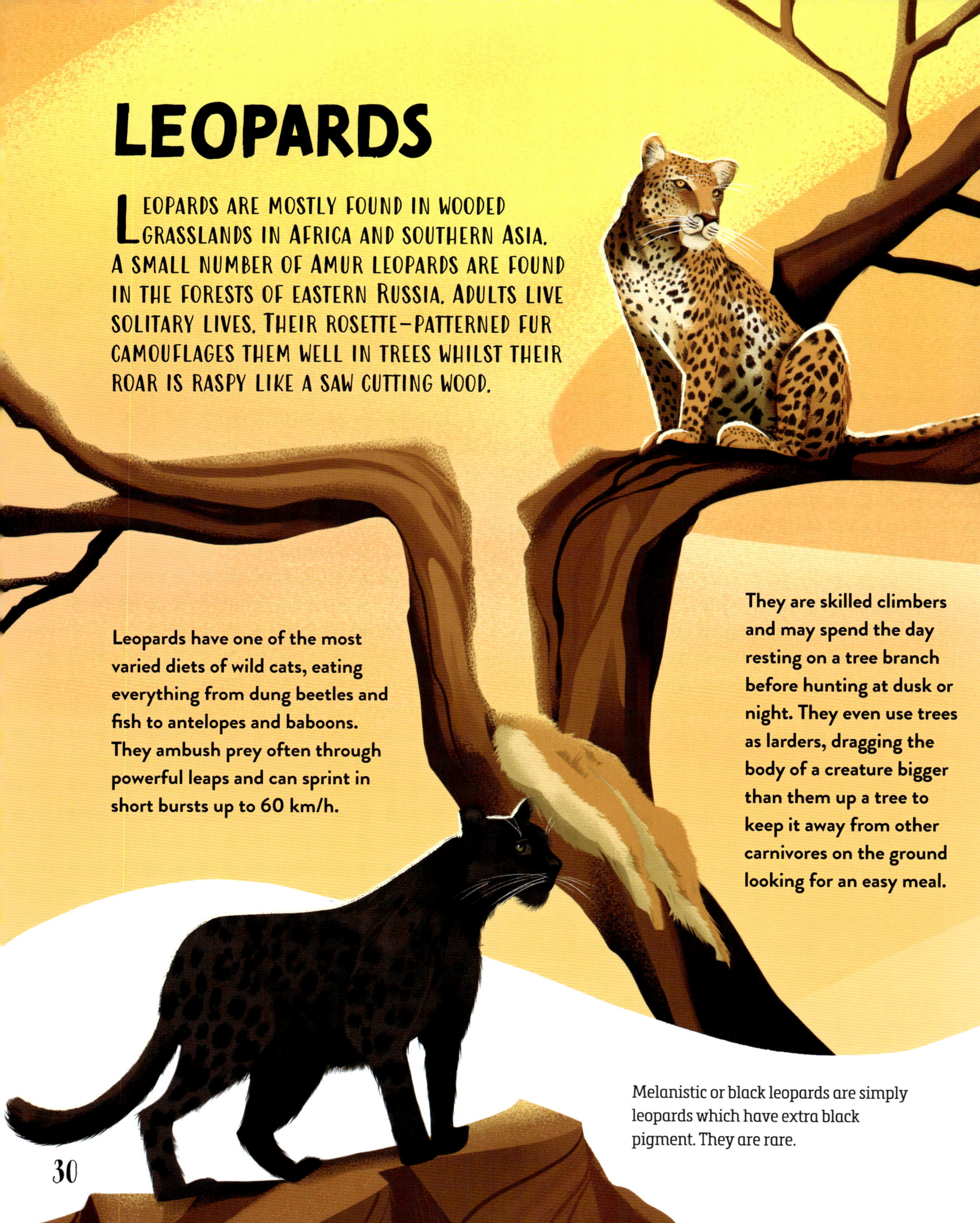

Melanistic or black leopards are simply leopards which have extra black pigment. They are rare.

SNOW LEOPARDS

THESE HIGH ALTITUDE CATS LOOK SIMILAR TO LEOPARDS BUT ARE ACTUALLY MORE CLOSELY RELATED TO TIGERS.

Their thick fur insulates them from the cold – a good thing as they mostly live in chilly mountainside regions in Asia. They go on marathon prowls using their short front legs and longer rear legs to clamber over rocky terrain. They can cover 20–35 km per night, on the hunt for sheep, deer or other prey.

Snow leopards are phenomenal jumpers, able to make leaps as long as 9 m.

MORE CATS

PUMAS

No cat is known by more names (mountain lion and cougar are two of many) or spread so widely as the powerful puma. These solitary animals are found throughout different parts of North and South America from Canada to Chile. Muscular and heavily built, they have great springing power and regularly leap onto prey to knock them off balance.

Pumas hunt mostly around dawn or dusk. They often bury part of a larger kill – covering it with leaves, dirt or snow – for a meal later.

OCELOT

Around twice the size of a domestic cat, these ambush hunters stalk the undergrowth of forests and bushlands in Central and South America. Their name comes from the ancient Aztec word, *tlalocelot*, meaning, 'field tiger'. Ocelots are good climbers and can be quite picky eaters.

European wildcats are nocturnal hunters mostly of rodents and rabbits.

EUROPEAN WILDCAT

Found in Spain, the Balkans and other parts of Europe, this is the only native cat living wild in the UK. It was once found throughout the British countryside but is now restricted to small, isolated parts of Scotland. The cat has a blunt, bushy tail marked with several black rings and its coat can grow thick and shaggy in winter.

DOMESTIC CATS

The domestic or house cat (*Felis catus*) is the most common species of cat worldwide. Some 11 million are kept as pets in the UK alone whilst many more stray and feral cats roam the streets and countryside.

More than 10,000 years ago, some peoples in the Middle East stopped wandering, settled down in one place and started growing crops. Early farmers found wild cats useful in keeping crop-eating pests like mice and rats under control. Over time, cats were kept as working animals, became domesticated and eventually evolved into the much-loved pets you know today.

Adult cats have an average head and body length of around 46 cm and weigh 4-5 kg. Maine coon cats are far bigger, weighing around twice as much. One Maine coon, called Stewie, measured 123.5 cm long.

Ragdoll

Abyssinian

Maine coon

The Maine coon is just one of more than 40 breeds of domestic cat. These are divided into long-haired (such as Persian, Scottish fold and Ragdoll), short-haired (including Siamese, Russian blue and Bombay) and one hairless breed, the Sphynx.

Bombay cat

Domestic cats tend to be playful and curious. Most can jump 3-6 times their body height and can make as many as 100 different sounds. They often form strong bonds with their owners.

Persian cat

Tabby cat

A young, healthy cat can sprint at a top speed of 48 km/h.

The average lifespan of a domestic cat is 13–15 years but some live for longer. A cat living in Texas, USA, called Creme Puff celebrated her 38th birthday in 2005.

Siamese

CATS AND HUMANS

Cats went from handy pest controllers to pets and gods in some ancient civilisations. Travelling on ships, where they kept mice and rats at bay, domestic cats were eventually spread around the world.

Ancient Egyptians started keeping cats around 4,000 years ago. Cats became associated with the goddess Bastet and were kept as pampered pets. Wealthy owners dressed their cats in silk and gold and let them eat from their own plates.

Statue of Bastet

When their pet cat died, some ancient Egyptian owners would shave off their eyebrows to show their grief. Thousands of dead cats were turned into mummies by their grieving owners.

In ancient China, farmers worshipped the cat god, Li Shou, who protected their crops from rats and drove away evil spirits.

Cats spread throughout Europe and Asia carried on trading ships and with invaders like the Romans and Vikings. European cats would endure tough times many centuries later in the Middle Ages where they become associated with the plague and witchcraft. Many cats were rounded up and killed.

Cats later travelled on the ships of explorers, navies and long-distance traders to reach North and South America and Australia. Some ships' cats were companions or symbols of good luck, but often the purpose was still practical, as mousers to protect food stored below deck from pests.

CATS IN CRISIS

The numbers in the wild of many species of cat are dropping fast. There are only a quarter of the lions there were 50 years ago and less than 7,000 cheetahs, 1,400 Andean mountain cats and 100 Amur leopards left. There are many reasons for these declines.

WHEN CATS ATTACK

Big cat attacks on humans are rare but do happen. Tigers, for example, killed 300 people in India between 2018 and 2022. Some 200 people in Africa die from lion attacks each year – less than half the number who perish due to hippos. Far more big cats, though, are hunted and killed by people out of fear or for profit.

Attacks on livestock by wild cats are more common and farmers and ranchers retaliate by shooting or catching cats in traps or wire snares.

POACHED FOR PARTS

Ocelots, leopards and many other beautiful wild cats are killed just for their fur. Other cats are caught, shot or poisoned so that poachers can make money selling body parts such as teeth, claws or internal organs. Tiger blood and powdered tiger bone, for example, are much-prized ingredients in traditional Chinese medicine whilst jaguar teeth and bone are equally valued in South America.

Andean mountain cats are endangered due to poaching for their own fur and by humans hunting chinchillas – the cat's most common source of food.

ILLEGAL WILDLIFE TRADE

Some rare cats are caught and sold to collectors and pet stores even though such transactions are against the law. Sometimes, adult cats are caught and traded, leaving their young cubs and kittens to perish in the wild.

LOSING THEIR HOMES

Cats in the wild need plenty of safe space to roam around in and a plentiful supply of animals to hunt. Both of these vital things are threatened when a cat's habitat shrinks, usually due to human activity.

Humans are rapidly reshaping wild landscapes. They are clearing vast areas of trees and bushes to create new farmland, cattle ranches, roads and settlements. Sometimes valleys are lost, flooded during the building of dams and hydro-electric power stations.

Deforestation is causing the loss of 12 football fields-worth of forest every minute, removing huge areas of key habitat for cats every year.

With less space to roam, cats find themselves in much closer contact with humans, leading to more being poached or hunted. Deforestation and roads can split territory up into lots of small patches which boxes cats in. Smaller habitats also reduce the amount of food available and may stop cats finding a mate to breed with, resulting in cat populations shrinking.

ENDANGERED EXAMPLE

Half of all the trees in the Indonesian island of Borneo have been cut down since 1970. This deforestation, a lot of it to clear land to grow oil palms, has removed much of the habitat of the bay cat which only lives on that island. Numbers of this small cat are dropping sharply. Less than 2,500 are now thought to exist.

HARMFUL HOMES

Some wild cats' homes haven't shrunk but they have been damaged and degraded. Dumped rubbish such as glass, plastics, wire and nets can entangle or injure cats. Chemicals and oil dumped into rivers pollutes water sources which may kill off the creatures cats rely on for food.

CAT STUDIES

Many people are trying to gain more knowledge about wild cat species so we can learn how to help them survive and prosper. Most cat species live solitary lives, are most active at night and are well-camouflaged in their surroundings. So, they can be very hard to spot and study.

Some researchers have turned to technology for help such as flying drones to track a cat's movements and discover the extent of its territory. They can also help count the numbers in a pride of lions, detect what young cats do when they leave their mother and the movements of a cat's likely prey.

Some big cats are caught, sedated and fitted with a tracking collar. This sends out radio signals and contains a GPS unit so that the cat's movements can be tracked in great detail.

Other naturalists rely on camera traps to capture vital data about smaller, more elusive cats. The digital cameras in a trap are triggered to take photos or video when their sensors detect the body heat or movement of an animal close by.

One cat conservation organisation called Panthera has set up 38,000 camera traps. Analysis of all these traps' photos and video give researchers more clues about how many cats are in an area and their behaviour.

Marbled cat

Injured cats or cubs and kittens that have lost their mother are sometimes taken into captivity and cared for at zoos and wildlife centres. They are studied as they heal and grow, and many are reintroduced back into the wild.

CAT CONSERVATION

Lots of work is being done to help conserve cats for future generations to enjoy. Many people are campaigning to stop the illegal trade in cats and their parts. Others are trying to prevent the further loss of or damage to cats' habitats.

Out in the field, game park rangers and wardens use drones, thermal imagers which can see people and cats at night and other techniques to try to stop or catch poachers. Not all methods are high tech; in Nepal, more than 400 local volunteers scan the land to find and remove snares and traps set by poachers to catch tigers.

The formation of more national parks, reserves and sanctuaries can give some cats a safe home to live in. So can establishing natural wildlife corridors between different wild areas that have been broken up by new farms and plantations. These allow cats and other animals to roam between habitats safely.

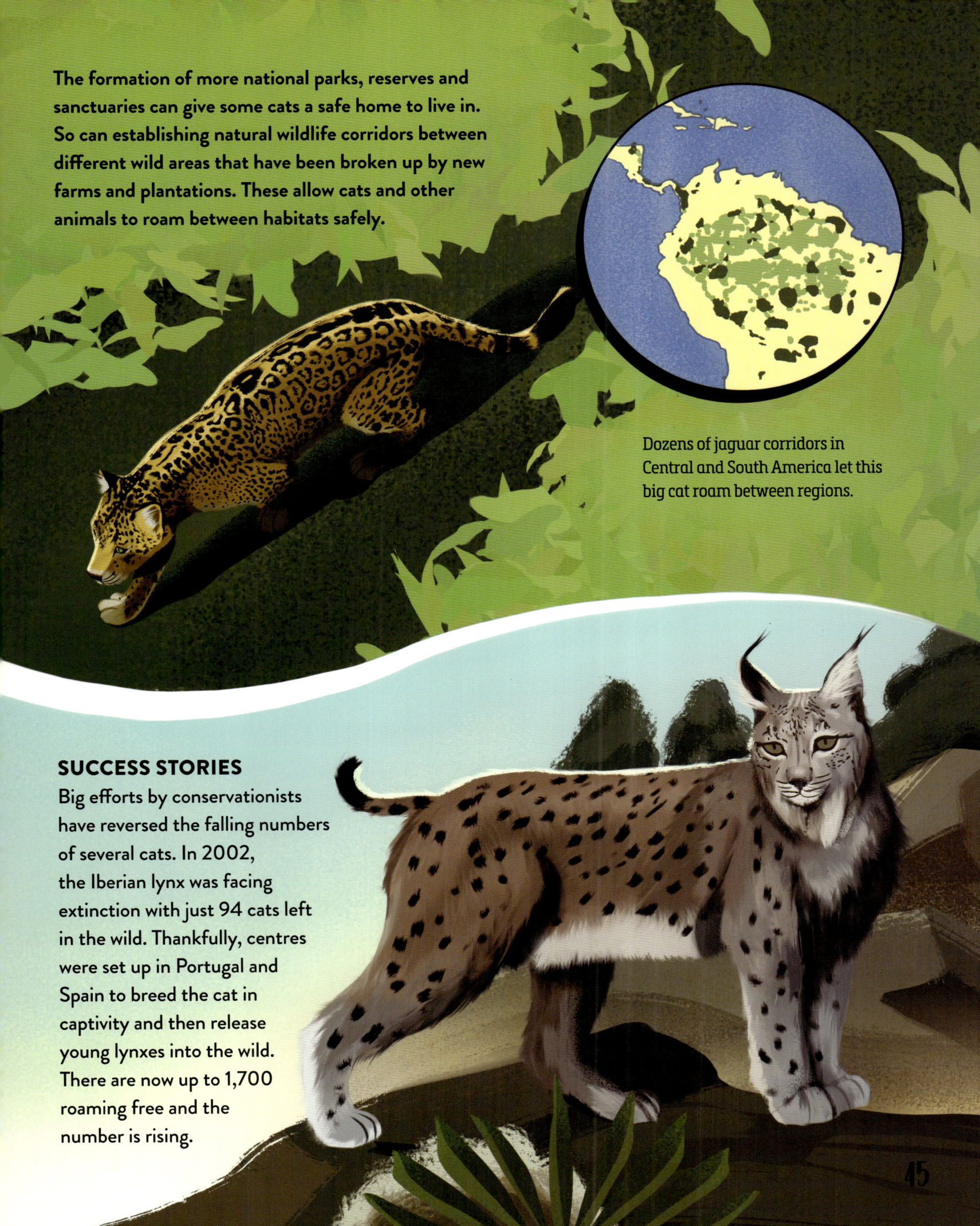

Dozens of jaguar corridors in Central and South America let this big cat roam between regions.

SUCCESS STORIES

Big efforts by conservationists have reversed the falling numbers of several cats. In 2002, the Iberian lynx was facing extinction with just 94 cats left in the wild. Thankfully, centres were set up in Portugal and Spain to breed the cat in captivity and then release young lynxes into the wild. There are now up to 1,700 roaming free and the number is rising.

GLOSSARY

Captivity When animals are kept by humans.

Carnivore An animal that eats meat.

Deforestation Clearing a large area of trees for the wood or to make room for farmland or settlements.

Drone A pilotless aircraft or helicopter, often remote-controlled from the ground by a person.

Extinct When a species of living thing dies out, never to return.

GPS Short for global positioning system, this is an advanced and accurate navigation system using space satellites to pinpoint a person or creature's location on Earth.

Groom When an animal keeps themselves, especially their fur, clean and tidy.

Habitat The natural home or environment of a living thing.

Insulate To surround or cover something to keep heat in.

Jacobson's organ A sense organ found in the roof of a cat's mouth.

Litter The name given to a collection of live baby cats.

Mummified A method preserving a dead person or animal by drying the body out and wrapping it in cloth.

Nocturnal A creature which, in general, is active at night and sleeps during the day.

Poaching To illegally hunt and catch or kill creatures without permission.

Predator An animal that hunts other animals for food.

Prehistoric The time before there was written or recorded history – stretching from about 6,000 years ago to millions of years.

Prey An animal hunted by another animal for food.

Pupil The dark, central part of an eye which lets light into the eyeball.

Rodents An order of mammals, most of which are small like mice and voles, and have large front teeth used for gnawing.

Savannah A large, flat plain with a lot of grass and scattered groups of trees, found on a number of continents especially Africa.

Scavenger An animal that seeks out and eats already dead creatures including those killed by other animals.

Sedated To give a person or animal a drug which makes them drowsy or fall asleep.

Species A group of animals that under normal conditions can have offspring together.

FURTHER INFORMATION

Books

A Book of Cats – Katie Viggers (Laurence King, 2021)

Cats (Happy Pet Friends series**)** – Katie Woolley (Franklin Watts, 2022)

Meet the Cats – Kate Peridot (Welbeck, 2024)

The Ultimate Book of Big Cats – (National Geographic, 2022)

Websites

www.thebigcatsanctuary.org/

The Big Cat Sanctuary is a charity dedicated to helping conserve big cats globally.

https://wildcatsmagazine.nl/wild-cats/

A fact-packed website with web pages on each species of wild cat.

www.youtube.com/watch?v=O4sS_-dR3Cc

Watch a cheetah in captivity break a speed record in this BBC video.

www.discoverwildlife.com/animal-facts/mammals/facts-about-big-cats

A great feature on big cats and their differences by Discover Wildlife magazine.

https://panthera.org/

A conservation website where you can learn more about many wild cats and what is being done to protect them.

INDEX

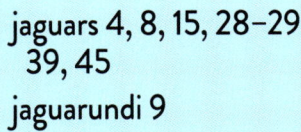

ancient Egypt 36
ancient China 36

bobcats 9

caracals 9
cats (types of)
  Andean mountain 38–39
  bay 9, 41
  black-footed 5
  fishing 11, 15
  flat-headed 9, 11, 21
  marbled 9, 43
  margay 15, 20
  Pallas's 9, 15
  pampas 5, 9,
  pet (domestic) 4–6, 9–10, 14, 16–18, 34–37
  sand 9, 20

cats
  anatomy 10–11
  evolution 6–9
  fur 14–15, 20, 31, 33, 39
  prehistoric 6–7
  senses 12–13, 21, 25
  threats to 19, 29, 38–41
cheetahs 9, 11, 15, 18, 26–27, 38
conservation, cat 43–45
cubs 10, 17–19, 23–24, 39, 43

grooming 17

hunting 4–5, 10–13, 15, 20–21, 23–25, 27, 29–31, 32–33

jaguars 4, 8, 15, 28–29, 39, 45
jaguarundi 9

kittens 10, 18–19, 39, 43

leopards 8, 15, 25, 30–31, 38–39
  clouded 5, 8, 14
  snow 8, 31
lions 4, 8, 15, 17, 22–24, 28, 38, 42
lynxes 10
  Canada 10
  Iberian 9, 45

ocelots 9, 15, 33, 39

pumas 4, 9, 32–33

scent marking 16
servals 9, 13, 21

tigers 4, 6, 8, 12, 15–16, 19, 24–25, 28, 31, 38–39, 44

wildcats, European 9, 18–19, 33